#1 SIMPLIFIED GUIDE FOR PAREN

MW00934923

A WINNING CUSTODY GUIDEBOOK

EVIDENCE STRATEGIES FOR CHILD CUSTODY

EVIDENCE STRATEGIES FOR CHILD CUSTODY

TABLE OF CONTENTS

DISCLAIMER

NOTHING CONTAINED HEREIN
SHOULD BE CONSTRUED AS LEGAL ADVICE.

All material and content in writing, images, audio, or video delivered via custodysimplified.com or fatheringfamilies.com, within the Fathering Families books, email, or personal coaching sessions are meant for informational purposes only and not intended to serve as (or be a substitute for) legal, financial, and/or tax advice. Use of the information and/or materials as a basis for any legal, medical, or financial decision by the user/reader is done strictly at the user's sole risk.

No warranties or representations of any kind are made to the user regarding the information and/or materials. No responsibility or liability is assumed by Fathers' Rights Simplified, Fathering Families, its employees, or affiliates. Laws may change over time and differ in your County, State, or Country. It is recommended that you seek counsel of a qualified attorney before taking any action. Please read the full Terms of Service.

FOREWORD

*Please note that the contents in this guide contain dialogue
and strategy advice directed towards fathers, but most readers
find the information to be applicable and extremely helpful to
any parent in a contentious child custody dispute.*

Often, a father's first obstacle to being an involved, active parent is
securing time with his children after a separation or divorce.
By guiding dedicated fathers on how to secure a fair custody
arrangement, this guide can help them set the stage for building
strong bonds with their children and being a positive influence on
their emotional, mental and physical well-being.

Evidence Strategies for Child Custody will assist dedicated fathers
in exposing the truth and gathering facts that support their child
custody case. In many cases, for a father to secure equal custody,
he must prove that he is a good, well-suited parent—if not the
better parent. Our goal is not to interfere with a mother's rights,
but to help committed fathers establish a strong negotiating
position for custody, empower them to obtain a balanced
parenting agreement, and secure an integral place in the
lives of their children.

INTRODUCTION

Most child custody guides focus very little on evidence collection, but understanding this aspect is vital for a parent to succeed. This book provides clear and concise guidance on how to gather evidence and properly prepare it based on critical custody factors, while also explaining what evidence could be used against you. Time with an attorney and in front of a judge is limited and costly. A parent's diligence in collecting evidence can save thousands of dollars, improve their negotiating position, and increase their attorney's efficiency in building a solid case.

The parent who wins a custody trial is often the one who is best prepared.

Fathers that take the appropriate steps to strengthen their case's position will find a greater opportunity to reach a settlement before the case has to be heard in the courtroom before a Judge. Study this guide and work with your attorney to develop an effective strategy for your particular case.

Properly organizing your evidence can save thousands of dollars and help your attorney's performance at trial.

THE GOAL OF EVIDENCE

In a child custody case, Judges often hear accusations from both parties. The goal of evidence is to support the claims made in your petition or testimony and defend yourself against accusations or lies presented in the opposing party's claims. Your case will be strengthened by evidence that either demonstrates your credibility or weakens the credibility of the other party.

When filing your pleadings or giving testimony, avoid lying or making any claims that you cannot support. Your credibility will be at risk.

Depending on your situation, you may spend more time collecting evidence that exposes the other parent or focuses on presenting yourself as a well-suited, active parent. In Family Court, lies are rampant, but accurately discrediting a fabricated testimony of an opposing party can significantly help your case as their subsequent claims begin to lose credibility.

Regardless of your desired custody arrangement, once a complaint for custody has been filed, your goal is to present a preponderance of evidence to demonstrate to the Family Court that you are the better-suited parent. For a father to be granted equal or primary custody, the Judge must feel confident that this custody ruling suits the best interest of your child.

OVERVIEW OF STEPS

When a relationship between parents is on the verge of dissolution, critical evidence can amass quickly as communication and interactions intensify with raw emotions. Whether you suspect that custody will be disputed by the other parent or you are currently in the legal process, it's important to start the evidence collection and organization process right away.

Time is of the essence. It is important to start gathering evidence immediately before an opportunity is lost or tracks are covered up.

1) Start gathering evidence

2) Create a relationship timeline

3) Begin using a journal with regular, dated entries

4) Understand what Family Court Judges look for

5) Develop a strategy supported by evidence

6) Categorize evidence by the "Custody Factors"

IMPORTANT TIPS

- Do not delete any emails, text messages, or voicemails
- Do not throw away written notes/letters, calendars, or receipts
- Be discreet with your collection process

STORAGE & SAFEKEEPING

A file storage box with hanging folders and handles is ideal for organizing and can easily be transported to your attorney's office or the courthouse. Print your documents and file them in relation to your case's strategy and the relevant "Custody Factors". These factors will be introduced and explained in an upcoming chapter.

You can avoid additional attorney fees by printing evidence documents yourself.

DIGITAL MEDIA

With the widespread use of computers and smartphones, a great deal of evidence is available via digital media. Emails, text messages, instant messages, videos, and photos can be easily backed up or stored on your computer and smartphone. For organizational purposes, take the following measures:

- Save emails in a PDF format. The timestamp and date of each email should be included in the email's header. Don't delete the original email in your inbox.
- Export text messages from your phone to your computer.
- Take screenshots of relevant online content, public postings, etc.
- If you export photos taken on your phone to a photo sorting program on your computer, make sure to save the original photo on your phone, as its original metadata will be intact and can further verify the photo's credibility.

- Label your photo and video files with a descriptive file name and date.
- Organize digital media in private folders based on evidence categories. Your evidence categories will be based on the Custody Factors.

BACKUPS

Frequent backups to an external hard drive or a portable thumb drive are critical. If your computer were to crash or your smartphone stolen, it could cost you a great deal of time or jeopardize your case. When possible, automate this backup process with Dropbox, an inexpensive, online service that automatically syncs specific folders on your computer to an online file storage account. An extra thumb drive is ideal for transporting your organized evidence files to your attorney's office.

PHOTO ALBUM

Buy a magnetic page photo album and begin storing photographs that clearly illustrate the home environment and your involvement with your child. Utilize this photo album as a way to demonstrate a healthy home life and an active relationship with your child. Any incriminating photographs of the opposing party should be stored separately in your evidence folders.

SAFEKEEPING

Store all items in a private location that is safe from damage or theft. Do not share your evidence with anyone other than your attorney or trusted individuals who are assisting in building your case. Evidence should be hidden from your child, houseguests, or the other parent and stored away from water, fire, or excess heat. If you are in a high-conflict case or have concerns about the safety of your evidence, consider a lockable, fireproof safe. Password protect your computer and phone for additional security.

> *During a child custody dispute, the security of your evidence is paramount.*

CREDIBILITY

For your evidence to be accepted by the Family Courts, it must abide by the basic Rules of Evidence, which state that it must be credible and not considered Hearsay or Privileged Communication. In most child custody cases, relevant evidence is admissible unless its probative value is outweighed by the danger of unfair prejudice, confusion of the issues, or by considerations of needless presentation of cumulative evidence, undue delay, or a waste of time. These are common evidentiary rules that apply to the bulk of legal proceedings, but in an effort to ascertain the best situation for a child, if a judge in the Family Court deems evidence or testimony relevant to the litigation, they may allow it.

To be credible, evidence must meet the following prerequisites:

1) It must be material
2) It must be relevant
3) It must be authentic
4) It must be timely

Don't waste the court's time with issues that don't have anything to do with custody or the best interests of your children.

PREREQUISITES OF CREDIBLE EVIDENCE

MATERIAL
The item should have a logical connection to a fact of consequence and significant to the outcome of a case.

RELEVANT
The item should have a tendency to make a fact more or less probable than it would be without presenting it as evidence and the fact is of consequence in determining the action.

AUTHENTIC
To effectively authenticate or identify an item of evidence, the proponent must present evidence that sufficiently supports a finding that the item is what the proponent claims it to be. Inventing or falsifying evidence is a crime.

TIMELY
The creation or occurrence of the item should originate within a relevant timeframe of the matters at hand. The Family Court may not consider a parent's lifestyle prior to the child's birth.

If you suspect your child is not in an appropriate living situation or is experiencing emotional or physical abuse while with the other parent, it is critical that you substantiate those concerns with credible evidence.

TYPES OF EVIDENCE

The most common types of evidence offered in a child custody case include: journals, emails, text messages, instant messages, voicemails, letters, greeting cards, photographs, videos, audio recordings, social media activity, schedules, and records (such as financial, medical, school, and police reports).

This chapter will elaborate on the important details that could be recorded and documented in these different types of evidence.

Never delete, discard, or misplace any of these items. Diligently gather, document, and file this information the moment you have concerns that custody could be disputed.

JOURNAL

When going through a heated custody dispute, it can be difficult to keep track of numerous events, but keeping a daily journal will be helpful for refreshing your memory and referencing details for your attorney. Journals entries can be handwritten logs, typed on the computer via a journal or notes app, or emailed to yourself.

Record events as soon as possible and write a brief summary of each day or interaction with the opposing party. Accompany each entry with the date and time. This may feel excessive at times, but this type of documentation can strengthen your case when accurate details are requested.

Helpful details to include in your journal:

JOURNAL ITEMS

EXCHANGES
- date, time, location
- tardiness
- contentious interaction
- any other issues, complications, delays in the logistics

PICK-UP & DROP-OFF LOCATION & SUMMARY
- daycare
- school
- after-school programs

MEALS
- what the child ate per meal
- general appetite
- likes and dislikes, favorite meals
- any allergies or aversions to specific foods

NAPS/BEDTIME
- length of sleep
- time they fell asleep
- quality of sleep session

DAILY ACTIVITIES
- playdates
- educational activities
- outings to the park/playground
- music practice
- sports, afterschool programs

JOURNAL ITEMS

CHILD'S BEHAVIOR & MOOD

- good or concerning behavior
- polite, patient, well-mannered
- attentive, communicative
- shy, withdrawn, anxious
- aggressive, disruptive, temper tantrums
- energy level (tired, disoriented, well-rested, calm, active)

HEALTH STATUS

- accidents or injuries and measures taken
- illness in either parent's care or upon exchange
- doctor and dentist visits
- reoccuring complaints

SCHOOL/EDUCATION

- homework status
- performance update
- behavior reports
- developmental milestones
- reports of tardiness or delinquent behavior
- incomplete or missing assignments

OTHER PARENT'S CONDUCT/INSTABILITY

- concerns about irresponsible parenting or neglect
- denial of communication or access to child
- violations of existing Custody Orders
- unilateral decisions
- resistance to co-parent

Daily journaling is important, even if your journal entry is: "Nothing significant to report today." These entries can offer insight into stable, daily routines and may help deflect baseless accusations.

Depending on the points of issues in your case, you will need to emphasize documentation in those areas. If you are in a high-conflict case or the other parent is a compulsive blamer, you will likely need to include additional detail to deflect incoming accusations. For example, if you are being accused of feeding your child a poor diet, you may need to include a list of lunch contents that you provided the child while they attended school or daycare.

Note:

Stick to the facts and be careful not to make unnecessary crude comments about the other parent in your journal. If you use it to refresh your recollection at trial, the other party can request a copy and the Judge could interpret any malicious statements as slanderous or aggressive.

EMAILS

Emails have become a ubiquitous method for communication and very effective evidence in Family Court since each header contains detailed information about the sender, recipient, date, and timestamp. Because email communication is often an informal exchange, people tend to write very candidly without realizing how damaging or misinterpreted the contents could be.

Email conversations can be exported to PDF files and saved into folders on your computer or printed and stored in the designated Custody Factor folder. Never delete the original email in your inbox. See the chapter titled Custody Factors & Your Strategy for more information.

TEXT MESSAGES

Similar to emails, text messages can be easily documented and are frequently used as evidence in Family Court. If you and the other parent use text messaging to communicate, use the same caution you would when using email and avoid emotionally driven, impulsive replies. Keep your phone safe at all times, back up the contents, and ensure that you can export your text messages to a printable file.

Emails and text messages can demonstrate a parent's demeanor or document active participation.

INSTANT MESSAGING

Skype, WeChat, LINE, Google and social media platforms offer real-time text communication online. Exporting chat history from these platforms depend on the program version you are utilizing. If you and the other parent use Instant Messaging to communicate, find out if your program allows you to capture past conversation logs. If you are communicating with the other parent on a platform that proves difficult to document, switch to email.

VOICE MESSAGES

Although some state laws prohibit the recording of telephone conversations, voicemail recordings that are left intentionally in your voicemail inbox or answering machine are generally admissible as evidence. When leaving a voicemail with the other parent during a custody dispute, speak in a mature manner and be mindful of your tone.

Note:

Intercepting voicemail to another party's inbox or gaining unauthorized access is a violation of federal and state wiretapping laws. Do not do this under any circumstance.

PHOTOGRAPHS

A well-curated photo album can demonstrate a safe home, healthy environment, and an active relationship with your child. Maintain a clutter-free home and take photos of the child's room and a clean play space. Include pictures of yourself and family members interacting with the child around the house, neighborhood, and at any community functions. Particularly while your custody ruling is pending, take candid photos that demonstrate your connection with the child and the wellbeing of your child while in your care.

If you have concerns that the child is victim to physical abuse or neglect while in the other parent's care, take pictures of any bodily injuries that are discovered right away and note details with the date and time in your journal.

VIDEOS

Similar to photos, videos of your home or you playing with your child can be useful to show the child's living environment and demonstrate your involvement before custody was disputed.

SPECIAL CASE - NANNY CAMS

In most states, parents can monitor the interaction between their child and their in-home childcare providers without prior consent when done in accordance with the law. Nanny Cams or Surveillance Camera recordings, absent of audio capability, are usually admissible evidence if installed on your own property or where you have been granted permission. Federal and state wiretapping laws prohibit cameras from being secretly placed where someone is entitled to expect privacy such as a bathroom.

AUDIO RECORDINGS

At times, it becomes very difficult to determine who may be telling the truth and if concerns are warranted. If your case is high-conflict, audio recordings of your interactions with the other parent can reveal behaviors that are difficult to show in written form. Audio recordings can capture their demeanor while in front of the child or material that deflects false allegations of abuse.

Consider recording exchanges or potentially volatile interactions with the other parent to help demonstrate to your attorney the type of problems you are experiencing. Remember to be discreet and conceal the device without muffling the audio detection.

Basic pocket-sized recording devices are inexpensive and many smartphones offer free audio recording applications. With either device, make sure you can download the audio files and store them in the proper folder.

You cannot intercept another party's conversation that you are not a part of, nor can you "bug" or hide a voice-activated recorder in someone's vehicle or private residence. The recording of telephone conversations is regulated by state and federal laws and is generally illegal; however, telephone conversations within some states extend the "one-party consent law".

Note:

It is essential that you do not stage an event to provoke the other parent into a conflict while recording. Tampering with the audio file or attempts of entrapment can work against your case.

Note:

Be mindful of federal and state laws that oversee electronic communications. In many states, audio recording is permissible if there's consent from at least one of the parties, per the "one-party consent law" of 18 U.S.C. 2511(2)(d). The basic rule is: Audio can be legally recorded if at least one person participating in the conversation has consented to the recording and your state recognizes the "one-party consent law".

VICARIOUS CONSENT - A RARE EXCEPTION

Some states have made it permissible to record interactions between the other parent and your children while in your absence if you have a genuine concern that your child is a victim of abuse or neglect. If your intention is questioned, you must be able to demonstrate to the judge that it was in the best interest of your children to consent to a wiretap. Understand the laws in your area before using any recording device.

INTERNET & SOCIAL MEDIA POSTS

Social networking sites have been quickly adapted as a major form of interaction. Publicly posted comments, messages, photos, and videos are finding their way into the Family Court as admissible evidence. A user's activity online can reveal quite a bit about their behavior and lifestyle. Once you are in a custody dispute, use extreme caution when posting publicly on social networking sites and assume your activity is being documented.

If the other parent is publicly slandering you or exhibiting concerning behavior online, take a screenshot that displays the post, their name, any additional comments, and the date/time of the post and/or comment. Do not instigate an argument online or get involved in the inappropriate behavior.

Note:

The Electronic Communications Privacy Act, the Stored Communications Act, and Federal wiretapping laws make it illegal to intercept or gain unauthorized access to another party's private communications or information. Information that has been posted publicly should have no expectation of privacy and it is, therefore, fair game as evidence.

HANDWRITTEN NOTES & LETTERS, AGREEMENTS, AND CARDS

Handwritten content created by the child or other parent from any point of your relationship should be saved. Greeting Cards or letters received before the relationship went sour can show your involvement and commitment to the family or even demonstrate the opposing party's adverse behavioral traits.

PREVIOUS PARENTING AGREEMENT(S)

It is common for parents to make parenting agreements that were never put into an official court order. If any agreements were created before custody filings were made, it would be beneficial to offer these as evidence, especially if the other parent begins to resist co-parenting or denies you access to your child.

SCHEDULES

Informal custody schedules can be very helpful to demonstrate the time you've spent with your child or counter the other parent's sudden change in position, which can be common once custody is disputed. A copy of a schedule created by you and the other parent can counter their argument that you had no parental involvement. Keep copies of any calendars or prior schedules that you have created and print any online schedules before they are deleted.

RECEIPTS

Receipts can help demonstrate your financial responsibility and commitment as a parent while documenting the average expenses for your child. Regardless of what phase you are in, locate and keep receipts of payments made for any medical, dental, educational, childcare, or other living expenses that pertain to your child. If child support is ordered, it is essential to keep proof of these payments.

MEDICAL RECORDS

Obtain copies of medical records from your child's routine check-ups or visits from times of injury or illness. If your child has maintained good health and hasn't suffered any injuries in your care, medical records can be submitted as testimony to that fact. If you fall victim to false allegations of abuse or neglect, an immediate check-up with the child's pediatrician can help disprove these claims and show your concern for the well-being of the child.

SCHOOL RECORDS

School records that contain good-standing report cards, notes from teachers or counselors, and updates from school events or parent-teacher conferences you have attended will strengthen your case as a well-suited and involved parent. It is important to maintain good contact and be in communication with the child's teachers about any behavioral or developmental concerns.

FINANCIAL RECORDS

Assembling information about your financial responsibility for the child and family can be helpful to demonstrate your commitment, involvement, and ability to provide. Be prepared to offer accurate and organized financial records if you are approaching the court regarding child support orders or alimony. These documents may include tax records, paychecks, bank statements, receipts, and bills.

POLICE RECORDS

If a parent has a criminal record, certain types of crimes may have an impact on custody rulings. Judges will consider crimes that call into question the fitness of a parent or their suitability as a role model. If the court has concerns about a child being in danger, the court may request the records of both parents before making a determination.

Any evidence obtained unlawfully, such as unlawful entry or an illegal wiretap, is inadmissible and you may be held liable.

THE BEST INTEREST
OF THE CHILD

When assessing the appropriate placement of a child, Family Court Judges use a guiding principle called, "The Best Interest of the Child". The criteria of this principle, commonly referred to as the "Custody Factors", include items pertaining to parenting skills, level of involvement, cooperation as parents, behavioral patterns, stability, living situations, and status quo.

Once a Judge has assessed the Custody Factors pertaining to a particular case, they will determine what kind of custody arrangement is in the best interest of the child. This principle supersedes the Tender Years Doctrine, which once greatly influenced the Judge's determination of custody for children in their early years.

CUSTODY FACTORS
&
YOUR STRATEGY

Custody Factors consist of positive and negative traits that have varying levels of importance or priority depending upon your custody case and the presiding Judge. Whether negative or positive, these Custody Factors will assist the Judge in making the appropriate ruling. When developing your case's strategy, filing pleadings, or presenting your case to the court, always demonstrate a genuine concern for the well being and best interest of your child.

The most effective custody case strategies emphasize the Custody Factors as they relate to the best interests of the child.

POSITIVE CUSTODY FACTORS

The following is a list of positive traits that you should emphasize, in effort to strengthen your custody case and improve the likelihood of a favorable custody ruling.

YOUR INVOLVEMENT

Be able to demonstrate that you are actively involved in your child's life from extracurricular activities to doctor visits. Take an active role in their mealtimes, daily routines, bedtime, schooling, outings, commitments, etc.
Show that you have a positive relationship and have substantially bonded with your child. If the other parent is interfering with your involvement, document your attempts and the resistance you are receiving.

HEALTHY & STABLE LIVING ENVIRONMENT

Present a safe, nurturing environment for your child, inside and outside of the home. Maintaining a clean, clutter-free home that offers the child their own bedroom and a safe play space can demonstrate a healthy, nuturing environment. Provide the child with regular, nutritious meals and keep a record of your grocery receipts. Take photos and short videos that clearly demonstrate the home life, environment, and the child while in your care. If you already live in a safe and nurturing home, it is preferable not to move during this time.

DEPENDABILITY

Always be on time for exchanges, pickups, and drop-offs. If the other parent is unreliable and often late, clearly document these occasions. Keep any correspondence with your ex that demonstrates your dependability, reliability, and commitment to your child's needs.

PARENTING SKILLS

It will be important for you to effectively demonstrate your responsible parenting skills to the Family Court. Depending on your case, you may need to highlight your competence in providing for your child's physiological needs (food, hygiene, sleep, safety, care), exercising proper discipline or behavior management, guiding and assisting their development (homework), positive role modeling (consistency, morality, patience), and having an emotionally healthy connection with your child.

Note:

Regardless of how diligent you are in documenting and gathering evidence of your parenting skills, if you aren't actively exercising good parenting your competencies as a parent may be vulnerable to accusations and criticism. When embarking on a custody battle, if you can improve or modify your behaviors that impact the child in positive ways, you should implement those changes immediately. Do not underestimate how much your ex can place your parenting skills in question.

ROUTINE & CONSISTENCY

Providing your child with a simple routine can make their world more predictable and stable. Consistent rules and structure will help them develop self-discipline and give them a sense of security. A Judge will feel more comfortable with a child living in an environment that offers a healthy routine with less anxiety or worries.

WILLINGNESS TO CO-PARENT

Although it may be an inner struggle, actively cooperating with the other parent will demonstrate your maturity, communication skills, and child-centric priorities.
Good co-parenting consists of openly and actively sharing parenting duties and decisions with the other parent, as well as important information about the child. Judges want to see that you are willing to make transparent, shared decisions about your children's activities and their educational and financial needs.

PROMOTE INVOLVEMENT OF THE OTHER PARENT

Demonstrate that you encourage the contact and active involvement between your child and their other parent. Unless clear evidence shows that the child is in danger while in their care, the Family Court will frown upon your interference with the child's relationship to their other parent. Don't encourage or instruct your child to call your significant other "Mommy" or "Daddy", as this can create tension and be interpreted as a form of Parental Alienation.

NEGATIVE CUSTODY FACTORS

The following is a list of traits that can negatively impact the outcome of a child custody case. If the other parent is actively engaging in any of the following negative Custody Factors, clearly document and incorporate this evidence into your case's strategy.

PARENTAL ALIENATION

The Judge's determination of the better-suited parent is influenced by identifying which parent is more likely to facilitate a frequent, continuing, and meaningful relationship between the child and the other parent. Parental Alienation is damaging to child's mental and emotional well being and it is taken very seriously by Family Courts. Document any behavior, conversation, or interaction with your ex (or their side of the family and friends) that slanders, denigrates or interferes with your relationship to your child.

UNWILLINGNESS TO CO-PARENT

If your ex is being uncooperative, making unilateral decisions, or withholding information such as your child's school or medical documentation, then they are not demonstrating an ability or willingness to co-parent. Major decisions and responsibilities concerning the child's development, education, and medical care should be openly discussed by both parents. Judges will be concerned about a parent that is reluctant to put aside their relationship issues and unwilling to co-parent amicably.

LOSS OF CONTROL & ANGER ISSUES

Emotional instability can surface and become more apparent during custody disputes. A parent who regularly loses control or is unable to manage their anger may be considered an unhealthy role model for the child. The child's home environment with this particular parent will be questioned. Angry outbursts in front of the child, teachers, neighbors, social workers, or court officials will be noted. Be very diligent when documenting any time the other parent is engaging in contentious behavior in the presence of the child.

Note:

Unfortunately, the actions of males are more easily construed as violent, aggressive, angry, or abusive. You must pay particular attention to your impulses, softening your communication and mannerisms during this time. Do not speak, write, or send anything (texts, emails, voice messages, handwritten letters) to your ex that may be easily misinterpreted as aggressive or threatening.

PSYCHOLOGICAL DISORDERS & MENTAL ILLNESSES

Parents with mental illnesses can put a child at risk by exposing them to a number of maladaptive behaviors while increasing their likelihood of developing similar disorders or behavioral issues. A large percentage of custody cases that actually go to trial involve at least one parent that exhibits signs of a personality disorder, making it very difficult to negotiate a fair settlement before trial.

Common disorders that show up in high-conflict child custody disputes are Borderline Personality Disorder, Narcissistic Personality Disorder, Histrionic Personality Disorder and Sociopathy. These psychological disorders can manifest as intense anger, violence, erratic mood swings, excessive blaming, or contentious, manipulative, vindictive, and impulsive behavior. Other mental illnesses or signs of instability that may impact a custody case include bipolar disorder, depression, or suicidal tendencies.

Note:

Custody cases that involve personality disorders require an assertive strategy. Personality disorders and psychological evaluations are discussed in more depth in a later chapter.

DRUG OR ALCOHOL ABUSE AND LIFESTYLE

In the effort to establish the most stable environment for the children, most Judges will take allegations of substance abuse very seriously and will generally order a drug test or grant a motion for one, if they believe that one or both of the parties seeking custody is using drugs. A Judge may determine that a parent who drinks irresponsibly or is frequently out "partying" to have a diminished capacity to care for the child and poses a potential risk for behavior that puts the child in danger, such as driving under the influence or neglect.

DOMESTIC VIOLENCE

If a parent has a history of domestic violence against the other parent, a child, or past domestic partner, a Judge may limit their visitation, order supervised visitation, or in severe cases, deny custody if it is believed that this parent poses a present danger to the child or other parent.

CHILD ABUSE AND NEGLECT

Physical harm, emotional harm, and neglect to a child by an adult are considered forms of child abuse. Parents have the responsibility to protect their children, which includes monitoring the behavior of assigned caretakers such as family members, friends, or romantic partners. If a parent disciplines their child through spanking, it may be considered child abuse. Even if it is legal in your state, it is advisable to not use corporal punishment during this time.

Four Major Categories of Child Abuse:

1. PHYSICAL ABUSE
Intentionally harming a child's body through bodily contact or forceful activity

2. SEXUAL ABUSE
Adult sexual behavior and engagement with a child including molestation, exploitation, or using a child for sexual pleasure

3. EMOTIONAL ABUSE
Belittling, rejecting, humiliating, isolating, terrorizing, or ignoring a child

4. NEGLECT
Omission of care resulting in, or risk of significant harm to a child

Physical
failing to meet basic living needs of the dependent, such as providing adequate food, clothing, hygienic living conditions, shelter, and safety

Emotional
failing to meet basic needs for attention, affection, and security

Educational/Developmental
failing to meet the intellectual needs of the child or state-mandated educational requirements

Endangerment
behaving recklessly while the child is in your care or exposing the child to hazardous living conditions

Medical
failing to tend to child's health-related, medical, or dental needs

Inadequate supervision or abandonment
when a caregiver fails to provide adequate supervision or leaves the child with an inappropriate caregiver or home alone at an inappropriate age. Many states offer guidelines with the Department of Health and Human Services or other child protective agencies on a child's ability to be left home alone. Factors include the child's age and their maturity level, the arrangements made to ensure the child's safety, and the overall safety of the surrounding area and circumstances.

Note:

When child custody is part of a separation or divorce, the situation can quickly become volatile. Unfortunately, while a parent's priority should be the child's best interest, it is common for abuse allegations to be used to restrict the other parent's access to the child.

If you are the target of false accusations of domestic violence, abuse, or negligent parenting, you need to develop a defense that counters the allegation and effectively demonstrates that the child is safe in your care.

INFIDELITY & NEW RELATIONSHIPS

Although adultery alone is rarely a weighted factor in a Judge's determination of child placement, the moral standards of a parent are considered. At times, infidelity can affect custody rulings if a parent has exposed the child to inappropriate situations or neglects the child due to irresponsible priorities and behavior. If a Judge determines that this behavior doesn't directly affect the well being of the child, it may not be considered by the Family Court.

Family Courts have varying perspectives about introducing a new romantic or living partner soon after the parents separate. Some conduct under these conditions may negatively affect the outcome of your custody dispute. Examples of detrimental conduct include: a parent shifting priorities away from the child and onto the new relationship, the new significant other poses a danger to the child, or abruptly exposing the child to the new relationship and provoking confusion.

Note:

If you include information regarding your ex's infidelity, new relationships, or cohabitation in your case for custody, make sure it relates to the child's best interest and does not come across as jealous or vindictive.

FALSE ALLEGATIONS, LYING, AND PERJURY

Lying during testimony or in pleadings is an extremely risky tactic that can cost a parent their credibility in court and even custody of their child. Do not write down any statements in court documents that you cannot back up with some type of proof. A parent who actively lies before the court will also put their parenting skills and competency into question. If you are dealing with multiple false allegations, gather specific information that demonstrates that these allegations are false, exaggerated, or misrepresented.

Submitting pleadings or other testimony that are laden with unfounded and unnecessarily inflammatory attacks can hurt your case. Avoid making wild or unsupported allegations.

Note:

Perjury (willfully lying under oath) is a crime, but it is exceedingly rare for criminal charges to be filed based upon perjury or false testimony in a Family Court proceedings. With the penalty of denying custody to a parent, it is believed that the Family Court has the necessary power to appropriately punish acts of perjury.

BLAMING AND SLANDERING

If the other parent is exhibiting signs of narcissism or other personality disorders, you will likely receive blame for everything imaginable. Regardless of the motivation, you will want to show a pattern of being unjustly and chronically blamed while they constantly project themselves as a "perfect parent".

Refrain from placing blame on the other parent or dramatizing yourself as the victim.

Although criticism from the other parent is often expected during a custody dispute, accurate documentation of their public slander campaign can reflect negatively on their maturity level or likelihood of encouraging an active and healthy relationship between you and your child.

*This list is by no means exhaustive. Consult your attorney to develop your case's strategy and which criteria to focus on for your case.

EVIDENCE PATTERNS

Your case's strategy should emphasize specific Custody Factors and any visible patterns. Well-documented evidence that clearly demonstrates patterns of concerning behavior affecting the welfare and best interest of the child will carry a lot of weight. Revealing the opposing party's behaviors that show a pattern of irresponsible or inappropriate behavior on a consistent basis will be more convincing to the Judge than pointing out a single judgment error. These patterns should be apparent in a relevant timeframe and illustrate the likelihood or tendency for it to continue to affect the child.

Unless it was a serious incident, emphasizing a single judgment error will not serve as very influential evidence.

Note:

Your evidence strategy does not have to make claims that the other parent is abusive or unfit, it can demonstrate that they do not have the time or the ability to provide an environment as suitable as you can, due to a busy work schedule, financial instability, or an unfit home.

ORGANIZING EVIDENCE

Many parents lump their documents together by evidence type, but a folder that's overloaded with emails or text messages differing in purpose and probative value will be a headache to your attorney and may delay opportunities for rebuttal during your trial. It is far more effective to organize your available evidence by the Custody Factors that support your case's strategy. Label evidence folders by Custody Factors such as, "Parent's Involvement" or "Parental Alienation".

Organize your evidence by custody factors, not by the type of evidence.

STEPS TO ORGANIZING YOUR PHYSICAL EVIDENCE DOCUMENTS

1) Purchase a file storage box and hanging files
2) Place an Evidence Index in the first folder for quick access
3) Label tabs on your hanging folders by your Custody Factors
4) Order the folders by prioritizing each applicable Custody Factor
5) Use labeled manila folders inside your hanging folder to keep documents together and organized

EVIDENCE INDEX

An Evidence Index of your documents, categorized by Custody Factors, will keep you organized while helping your attorney build a strong case and have a quick reference to your exhibits during trial. This index will serve as a high-level outline that emphasizes important issues impacting your case.

(example)

EVIDENCE INDEX

Plaintiff: Erik Dearman

Defendant: Angela Smith

Example Categories: (Based on Custody Factors)

1. Father's involvement
2. Living environment
3. Parental Alienation
4. False allegations
5. Mother's unwillingness to co-parent
6. Psychological issues or concerns

If you have the time, you will want to create an Evidence Summary with additional details and specific instances. Include a brief description of each Custody Factor and how it pertains to your case. You can't always rely on your attorney to remember all the fine details and the evidence summary can be a helpful reminder of your situation before trial.

(example)

EVIDENCE SUMMARY

Plaintiff: Erik Dearman
Defendant: Angela Smith
Categories: (Custody Factors)

FATHER'S INVOLVEMENT

Summary:

Father has been actively involved with parenting the child since birth. He regularly partakes in meal preparation, bedtime routine, homework assistance, and transporting the children to/from school and extracurricular activities. He tends to the child's emotional and developmental needs. He also takes financial responsibility for their educational needs, as well as medical and dental care.

Evidence: (Include Type of Media and Facts Only)

- Email confirming Father as child's soccer coach. (Date)
- Emails about father-son camping plans, (Dates)
- Recent teeth cleaning bill. (Date)

- Text messages about Teacher Conference attendance, (Date)
- Photo Album - Pictures of the father and child playing in the park, building a fort, fishing, playing in the backyard, playing in the snow, cooking together, (Dates)
- Meals documented in father's journal (Dates)

PARENTAL ALIENATION

Summary:

Mother has confused the child about the identity of their biological father by instructing the child to refer to her new boyfriend as "Daddy". Mother criticizes the father in the presence of the child and interferes with the father's time and relationship with child.

Evidence: (Include Type of Media and Facts Only)

- A witness statement from a neighbor who heard the mother calling her new boyfriend "Daddy" in front of the child, (Date)
- Recording of the mother telling the child during an exchange, "Your father is mean and he just wants to make mommy sad.", (Date)
- Text messages of the mother denying the father's time with child by presenting unacceptable excuses, (Dates)
- Text messages of the mother refusing to disclose the whereabouts of the child, (Dates)

Note:

These Evidence Indexes will be placed in the front section of your storage box for easy reference and the subsequent folders should be labeled with the designated Custody Factor.

WITNESSES

A witness is a person who provides testimonial evidence, either orally or written, of what he or she knows or claims to know about an event or matter relative to the case. Witness testimony can assist the Judge in determining the legitimacy of said claims and allegations in a child custody case. The most influential testimonies come from an unbiased witness that has personal or expert knowledge of both the child and/or the parents. There are various types of witnesses, but in Family Court proceedings, testimony generally comes from a factual witness, expert witness, or character witness.

FACTUAL WITNESS (WITNESS OF FACT)

A Factual Witness has personal knowledge about a matter of interest to the court - most commonly, about an incident that was personally heard or seen. A witness of fact offers observational testimony (by a recitation of the facts) about matters that he or she has perceived directly through their senses: seen, heard (as opposed to hearsay), touched, tasted, or smelled. Factual Witnesses cannot offer their opinions or assumptions in their testimony.

EXPERT WITNESS

A witness may only testify as an expert if he or she is qualified to do so. This qualification is received through one's study, practice, education, experience, or observation that has resulted in a professionally recognized expertise in a subject relevant to the case. In order for the Family Court to consider a witness to be an expert witness, the party presenting the witness must qualify them by asking the witness a series of questions that will help demonstrate what special knowledge the witness possesses. Based on the factual evidence that has been presented in court, Expert Witnesses are permitted to express their professional opinion or provide a diagnosis of the subjects within their area of expertise.

Requesting the testimony of professionals in some fields may require a fee or retainer and their reimbursement of travel expenses. Expert witness testimonies can greatly influence a Judge's custody ruling and, for this reason, the expense of offering this kind of testimony may be worth the investment in a high-conflict child custody dispute.

In child custody cases, the following professionals commonly offer expert testimony:

- Mental Health Practitioners
- Psychologists or Psychiatrists
- Pediatricians or other Medical Specialists
- Guardian ad Litem
- Social Workers
- Custody Evaluators

Note:

A Custody Evaluator's recommendation or opinion can carry substantial weight in the outcome of a child custody case. If the Judge has ordered that you be evaluated by a Custody Evaluator, it will be necessary to prepare yourself and your home. In a contested case, most states require the agency or person making the evaluation to furnish copies of the study for the attorneys of each party when it is completed or sufficiently before the date of commencement of the trial.

CHARACTER WITNESS

A character witness testifies on behalf of your character or reputation. When selecting character witnesses to support your case, choose people that can speak about your good ethical and moral qualities and have first-hand knowledge of your parenting, your relationship with your child, or your positive reputation in your neighborhood, community, church, etc. Friends and family are admissible as character witnesses, but their likelihood of bias and personal stake in the outcome may discount the value of their testimony. When possible, try to select third-party objective witnesses such as teachers, coaches, pastors, etc., who are active in your community and can affirm your stability, moral character, responsible parenting, and/or involvement in your child's life.

CHOOSING YOUR WITNESS

When considering witnesses for your case, start by making a list of individuals that have observed you with your child firsthand. People who have had recent and frequent contact with you and your child can provide a stronger testimony to support your case. Depending on the issues involved, you may need a variety of witnesses. Helpful witnesses might include:

- Teachers who have overseen the child within the last two grade years
- Daycare providers, babysitters, nannies
- Medical Providers that have treated or examined the child
- Therapist or other counselor observing or treating the child
- Coaches, parents, or other adults in your community that have assisted with your child's extra-curricular activities
- Friends or family members who have frequent contact with you or your child
- Your pastor, minister, rabbi, etc
- Social workers who have had contact or been involved with your family or case

Before the trial date, your attorney should have contacted and counseled your non-expert or character witnesses so they are prepared for any questions that might arise. If your supportive witnesses are not normally required to dress professionally, remind them to dress business casual, wear minimal jewelry or visible body piercings, cover their tattoos, and be well-groomed. Showing respect to the court can influence how the Judge perceives them and their testimony. Even if the person has been subpoenaed, send them a pre-trial reminder containing the time of the hearing, location of the courthouse and courtroom, and parking information.

SUBPOENAS

If you want someone to testify for you at your hearing, but have concerns about whether or not they will come, you should subpoena this person as a witness. A subpoena is a summons that legally requires an individual to appear in court to give testimony or bring forward certain documents as evidence. Often a person will agree to attend the hearing without a subpoena, but work schedules, time conflicts, or even the controversial nature of a child custody case can dissuade people from voluntarily testifying. If you do not serve the subpoena in advance and the person does not come to the hearing, you may be required to proceed without the potential benefit of their testimony or evidence.

If your trial is postponed or delayed, a witness will generally be provided an alternate date and time of appearance and will remain under legal order to appear when requested. If you have an essential witness, consider checking if witness subpoenas in your district are re-validated automatically. In some courts, witnesses can request a reimbursement to cover their loss of income or travel expenses.

EXAMINATION

During a court hearing or trial, lawyers may call upon witnesses to give testimony based upon what each one has heard or observed that is relevant to the case and matter at hand. Before the questioning begins, the witness must take an oath, to tell the truth under penalty of perjury. Direct Examination is the first round of questions and begins with the plaintiff's attorney directing the questions. The opposing counsel will then cross-examine the witness to undermine or impeach the witness' credibility or said claims, with the goal of demonstrating that the witness is biased, lying, unreliable, or has some personal stake in the outcome. An attorney cannot ask "leading" questions during direct examination, which suggest an answer; however, an attorney's cross-examination can pose questions that may suggest or imply an answer.

After the cross-examination, the plaintiff's attorney has an opportunity to ask the witness additional questions to further clarify their account. As a parent, you can also be considered a witness and will be subject to the same procedures if called to testify.

WITNESS WORKSHEET

It is important to provide your attorney with the names and contact information of your witnesses early on in your case, offering them sufficient time for preparation or necessary interviews. In addition to this information, you should confirm their profession, your connection or relationship to them, what kind of withness they are (expert, factual, or character), and a brief explanation of the knowledge they have to support your case.

(example)

WITNESS FULL NAME: Julie Marie Overstreet	**PHONE NUMBER:** (555) 555-1212 **ADDRESS:** 3355 Main Street Mill Valley, CA
PROFESSION: Project Manager at AMR Technologies	**RELATION/CONNECTION:** Friend, Care Provider
TYPE OF WITNESS: ☐ Expert ☐ Factual ☑ Character	**BRIEF EXPLANATION:** Why is the witness important? What does the witness know? How can this witness support the elements? How does the witness help the overall "story"?
WITNESS FULL NAME: Aimee McMann	**PHONE NUMBER:** (555) 555-3232 **ADDRESS:** 6645 Walnut Avenue San Francisco, CA
PROFESSION: Clinical Psychiatrist	**RELATION/CONNECTION:** Child's therapist
TYPE OF WITNESS: ☑ Expert ☐ Factual ☐ Character	**BRIEF EXPLANATION:** Why is the witness important? What does the witness know? How can this witness support the elements? How does the witness help the overall "story"?

OUT OF STATE WITNESS TESTIMONY

It can be cost-prohibitive to transport and accommodate a critical witness that lives a considerable distance away. If a witness resides out of state or is unable to travel a long distance, you may be able to arrange for testimony by phone or via audiovisual means. You will still need to arrange a proper venue and retain the services of a court reporter to be present. For depositions taken with witnesses that cannot appear in court, it is advisable to arrange videotape recording with the court reporter services in advance.

AFFIDAVITS

There will be times when documents submitted as evidence to the court will require a sworn statement to verify that the enclosed information is accurate to the affiant's knowledge.

This document, known as an affidavit, is a voluntarily-produced statement that contains facts or information believed to be true by the person producing the statement, the affiant. An affidavit is then notarized or authenticated under penalty of perjury, attesting that the affiant personally appeared before the authenticating party.

An affidavit is a declaration usually made in lieu of oral testimony, without any cross-examination and therefore only encompassing information "as the drafter sees them" and not necessarily considered an objective fact. An affidavit's weight or impact may differ from that of oral testimony. Depositions and in-court examinations of witnesses allow for a cross-examination opportunity whereas affidavits do not.

Documents or evidence that may need to be accompanied by an Affidavit may include:

- Pleadings submitted to the clerk of court
- Financial documents
- Witness statements
- Character reference (Affidavit of Character)
- Physician's report (Physician's Affidavit)
- Psychological Evaluations

AFFIDAVITS OF CHARACTER

An effective affidavit of character should succinctly convey your good moral character and behavior, indicating that you are a responsible, well-suited parent. Ideally, it is written by a witness that has had recent experiences with you and your child on multiple occasions. When thinking of who should submit an Affidavit of Character on your behalf, choose wisely.

An Affidavit of Character should present the following information:

1) Date of written statement.

2) Name of presiding Judge and address of the Family Court overseeing the case.

3) Professional Salutation: Dear (Judge's Name) or "To whom it may concern,"

4) *First paragraph:* Includes self-introduction and defines the relationship to the parent.

5) *Second paragraph:* Elaborates on the parent's personality, character, trustworthiness, and responsible nature.

6) *Third paragraph:* Includes brief, relevant anecdotal evidence that supports the above claims. (For example, a short explanation about how their child attended a sleepover party at the Plaintiff's home and not only did they witness how very attentive and considerate the parent was to all the young guests, but their child had a really positive experience and really looked forward to the next time they're invited over.)

7) *Final paragraph:* A succinct statement that supports the parent's request for child custody and the best interest of the child.

8) Signature and full name.

Judges want to see objective declarations that include statements of who, what, when, and where. Ask your references to stick to the facts rather than make emotionally driven claims. Testimonies that are clearly biased can be useless and waste useful time in front of the Judge.

HEARSAY RULE

Hearsay is commonly understood as a rumor, gossip, or statement that cannot be supported by a witness' personal testimony and are generally inadmissible in the courtroom due to its lack of reliability and trustworthiness. The Supreme Court defines Hearsay as a "testimony given by a witness who relates, not what he knows personally, but what others have told him, or what he has heard said by others".

The Hearsay Rule states that out-of-court statements are not admissible unless the truthfulness of the statement is irrelevant to the matter asserted, the original speaker is subject to an in-court cross-examination, or it falls under an exception to the Hearsay Rule.

Parents often have the urge to offer their children's statements as evidence. If a Hearsay statement is offered as evidence in the court, the opposing party has the right to object to the statement being heard before the Judge on the grounds that it is Hearsay.

HEARSAY EXCEPTIONS

If a Hearsay statement would benefit your case, you may be able to argue that it should be permissible based upon an exception to the Hearsay Rule. Although exceptions to the Hearsay Rule may vary from state to state, there are particular exceptions that may apply to child custody litigation. Coordinate with your attorney and presiding state laws to see if a particular out-of-court statement could be considered an exception to the Hearsay Rule.

Note:

Some things look like hearsay but aren't. In order to constitute hearsay, a statement must be "offered to prove the truth of the matter asserted". If the speech or conduct that is being testified to is *supposedly* being offered for a different purpose than proving that its content was true, then the court may conclude it is not hearsay at all. 1

Hearsay is one of the largest and most complex areas of evidence and therefore an understanding of the rule will be helpful in your evidence collection. The box below offers an explanation of the Hearsay Rule's application in Family Court proceedings.

The "Hearsay Rule" and its Applications (abridged)

If you are a self-represented party in a contested dissolution or child custody proceeding (or any other family law matter), it may be useful for you to become a familiar with the concept because it can be a critical sword for getting evidence that you consider favorable to your case in front of a judge or court commissioner, or as a shield to block claims from the other side that you don't want the court to hear or consider. Indeed, the hearsay rules have particular application in family law because much of such litigation involves accusations and counter-accusations that go on endlessly, many of which are quite "over the top" in terms of their tone and substance. Since live witness testimony must be taken upon request in domestic violence cases, this is often an area where it is critical for people without lawyers to have a basic understanding of the rules of evidence.

Some divorce litigants feel that they can say whatever they want, or use hearsay in a hope of inflaming bias in a judge to obtain what the litigant hopes for, and that even if a court sustains an objection to the hearsay (and "strikes" the statement(s) from the record) a bell has been struck that will continue to ring into the future in terms of a court's impressions of you. And, unfortunately, there is some truth to this - which is a good reason for knowing what to do with it at the outset.

Hearsay in family court proceedings is quite commonly found in declarations filed by the parties in connection with motion or OSC requests (order to show cause), whether these consist of the parties' own statements or the statements of third parties. Affidavits or statements "under penalty of perjury" are themselves hearsay.

The problem with hearsay evidence is that it is frequently unreliable and hence untrustworthy. Court's can't watch the demeanor of the declarant at the time they made the statement, and people, unfortunately, have all kinds of incentives to lie, minimize or exaggerate. While you need to fit your objections or the hearsay evidence you hope to introduce into a recognized exception to get it admitted, remember that the key is do everything in your power to show why the testimony can, on balance, be trusted. Knowing these rules can be an effective weapon for getting evidence excluded that you disagree with or find unfavorable. Often the other party has no idea how to respond, which is one good justification for the money that lawyers charge.

Thurman W. Arnold III (2012, Feb 12).
An Overview of the "Hearsay Rule" and Its Applications
Source: http://www.thurmanarnold.com/

RELATIONSHIP TIMELINE

Often, an entirely different picture can be presented based on the order of events. In addition to an Evidence Index, creating a relationship timeline that chronicles major events will refresh your memory and aid you in effectively communicating the circumstances to your attorney or during the trial. As soon as you have concerns about a custody dispute, begin creating a timeline of your relationship history with the other parent. Continue to document the changes in your relationship until the dispute is officially settled.

An effective timeline includes the dates of when the relationship began, residential history, birth dates of the children, career changes, instances of infidelity or abuse, breakups, marriage dissolution, when custody was first disputed, or other major milestones that relate to the family, child custody, and your relationship to the other parent. A relationship timeline paints an overall picture, whereas a journal is more commonly used to document and reference specific details on an ongoing basis.

RELATIONSHIP TIMELINE

Dec 11, 2009   Erik and Angela meet in Sacramento, CA.

Feb 1, 2010   Erik and Angela begin dating exclusively.

April 10, 2010   Angela moves into Erik's 1-bedroom apartment in Boulevard Park, Sacramento, CA after she is laid off from her job as a Teacher's Assistant.

July 15, 2010   Erik and Angela are engaged to be married in October 2010.

Oct 21, 2010   Erik and Angela's wedding in Cancun, Mexico.

Nov 11, 2010   First child is conceived.

July 20, 2010   Erik and Angela move into a 2-bedroom apartment in Berkeley, CA for Erik's job relocation at the University. He works feverishly to financially support the upcoming birth of their first child.

Aug 5, 2011   Erik and Angela's son is born in Berkeley, CA.

Aug-Sept 2011   Erik takes 4 weeks off of work to assist Angela with caring for their newborn.

Dec 2011   Angela is exhibiting extreme mood swings from rage to deep depression. Erik expresses concern for the well being of their son during these episodes. Angela is combative and begins limiting Erik's one-on-one time with their child.

Jan 16, 2011   Arguments continue to escalate when Erik expresses concern about Angela's mood swings and how it's affecting their child. Angela hits Erik while he is driving with the child in the back seat.

RELATIONSHIP TIMELINE

Feb 1, 2011

Angela begins taking their child to undisclosed locations for an extended period of time, sometimes overnight.

April 15, 2011

Erik discovers Angela spending intimate time with another man, Doug Reynolds. Angela admits that she is being romantic with Doug and has introduced their son to him.

May 20, 2011

Angela decides to move out at the end of May and move in with Doug. Angela proposes a schedule that only allows Erik every other weekend with their son. She threatens Erik that if he disputes this arrangement, she will offer even less time. Erik follows this schedule out of fear of not seeing his child.

July 22, 2011

After weeks of limited access to his son and many unilateral decisions made by Angela, Erik files for custody, requesting joint 50/50 custody.

It's important to continue keeping a timeline during the pendency of your case.

At the outset of the case, it is unlikely that you will have gathered and organized all the available evidence sufficiently enough to present to an attorney. However, a relationship timeline is an easy-to-produce document that will help you recollect of major events and assist your attorney in building a strategy at the outset.

Note:

If you intend for supporting documents, such as a Relationship Timeline or journal notes, to be only in the hands of your attorney, write the label "Notes to My Attorney" very clearly in the document's header. This will protect it from being subpoenaed.

WORKING WITH
YOUR ATTORNEY

Ensuring that your counsel has your evidence and can use it effectively requires a strategy relative to the Custody Factors, proper organization, and an understanding of how your attorney prefers to receive updates as new evidence becomes available. Working efficiently with a Family Law attorney requires discernment of which information to provide them immediately and which information should be held until it can be batched with supportive evidence.

INITIAL CONSULTATION

Your initial consultation with an attorney is usually to determine if they are a good match for your case, rather than developing a case strategy or presenting specific evidence. However, there are some essential items that you should prepare for these meetings.

- Summary of your circumstances and events related to your request for child custody
- Any separation agreements or court orders
- An idea of your preferred outcome and where you're willing to compromise

- Basic personal information of all parties involved (names, ages, contact details)
- Questions regarding their legal services (experience, specialties, availability, fees)

If you have time to gather this information before your initial consultation, the additional documents below may assist an attorney in understanding your situation.

- Financials (tax returns, list of major assets, liabilities, etc.)
- Employment Information
- Your Relationship Timeline

STRATEGY CONFERENCE

Once you have retained an attorney and sufficiently communicated the circumstances, you should discuss the Custody Factors that are applicable to your case and an initial strategy to consider while you gather and accumulate evidence. If the other parent's pleadings or counter-claims have been filed, this will be critical information to use when developing your strategy and defense.

If you've followed the suggestions presented in this guide, you will be more familiar with the Custody Factors and have your evidence more professionally organized than most attorneys' clients. Let your attorney know you will be collecting and organizing evidence around these factors and delivering the following items with your available evidence:

EVIDENCE PACKET

- Evidence Index & Summary
- Relationship Timeline
- Witness Worksheet
- Photo Album
- Video and/or Audio Recordings (if available)

If you've selected a good Family Law attorney, chances are they are juggling many other custody cases. You should not expect your attorney to remember all the details of your case without a properly prepared evidence packet that contains the items above.

ATTORNEY COMMUNICATION TIPS

Be discerning, non-impulsive, and organized

It is advisable to be discerning with how often you contact your counsel. Unless it's an urgent matter such as a court deadline, harassment from the opposing party, or you or the child are in danger, avoid excessively calling or emailing your attorney each time new evidence is accumulated or questions arise. If possible, wait until you can lump questions or concerns together and deliver evidence in a well-organized email before a scheduled meeting with your attorney. This will avoid unnecessary legal fees or annoying your attorney with unorganized information.

Note:

If you believe that you are in a critical situation or have information that needs immediate attention, contact your attorney accordingly.

Don't withhold evidence

Always be honest and forthcoming with your attorney. Withholding information may impair their effectiveness in preparing your case or cause a setback from of being caught off guard.

Any personal criminal history, drug use, or other negative custody factors that are likely to be brought up by the opposing party should be communicated to your attorney. The evidence that the other parent has against you may impact the position your attorney will take.
Be ready to answer the question: "What is the worst thing the other parent might say about you?"

Be Timely

Any requests made by your attorney for a meeting, more information, documents, signatures, or evidence should be a top priority. When your Family Law attorney is working on your case or developing a strategy, providing them information in a timely manner during this cumbersome process is essential and may save you money on attorney fees in the end. During the custody dispute, there will be important deadlines for filing documents that cannot be overlooked.

Note:

Your attorney's fees will likely be the largest single expense during the course of the process. Being organized, efficient, and discerning when communicating with your attorney will reduce the amount of information they need to sift through, the time spent compiling your case, and your overall cost.

Note:

If you can afford it, you may find the need to "shop around" for a Family Law attorney that not only is the right fit for your case but truly feels trustworthy and dependable. It's wise to read client reviews and to reach out to the positively rated attorneys in your area to schedule an initial consultation. Just one consultation with a popular or top-rated Family Law attorney, even if you don't intend to retain them, will automatically prevent the opposing party from meeting with or retaining that attorney.

Seek out an attorney with litigation experience if your case is high-conflict. Attorneys with litigation experience will not only have a pulse on the court's calendar system, but they'll also have a grasp on which Judges are fair to fathers requesting custody and/or favorable to joint custody outcomes.

EXCHANGES & INTERACTIONS

As stated earlier, if you are concerned about child custody being disputed or a dispute is in-process, be very cautious when conversing with the other parent face-to-face, over the phone, or online. Whenever you communicate in a format that can be easily documented, do not speak or write in any way that can be easily misinterpreted or construed as hostile or erratic.

When communicating with the other parent:

- Always remain calm and soften your mannerisms
- Show support for the other parent's involvement, if appropriate
- Speak in terms of the **best interests of your child**
- Avoid excessive finger pointing, blaming
- Your motives should not be driven by jealousy or revenge
- Assume anything you speak or write will be recorded or documented

If your custody case is high-conflict, take the necessary precautions:

- Avoid Traps - Never put yourself in a position where you can be falsely accused of physical abuse, violent tendencies, or verbal abuse. Do not accept any invitations that lure you into private residences or non-public locations with the other parent.
- Consider keeping physical contact with the other parent to a minimum or have a witness by your side during interactions.
- Utilize a recording device or a voice recorder app on your phone during in-person interactions. When you are recording, be especially mindful of your verbal exchange and keep the recording device concealed. Check with your presiding state laws before using a recording device to capture evidence.

EXCHANGES

Child Exchanges carry a high potential for conflict during a child custody dispute. Take these necessary steps to lessen the potential for conflict during exchanges or to help deflect false accusations.

- Arrange for exchanges, drop-offs, and pick-ups to be in public locations. If possible, have a witness with you.
- Briefly document each interaction or exchange in a daily journal or timeline, noting any conflicts or tardiness.
- Avoid contentious topics in the presence of the child.
- Directly after receiving the child in your care, observe them and take note of any new injuries, illnesses, or concerning behavior. It is possible that you could be blamed for an accident, illness, or injury that happened to the child prior to being in your care.

PERSONALITY
DISORDERS

Recent studies have reported that high-conflict custody cases have a higher likelihood of at least one parent with Borderline Personality Disorder (BPD), Narcissistic Personality Disorder (NPD), Sociopathy, or a related condition. People with BPD have an ability to maintain a public persona that appears very charming, but when triggered, cornered, or behind closed doors, they are vindictive, manipulative, and abusive to their spouse and have little empathy for the impact their behavior has on their child.

Parents who exhibit Borderline Personality Disorder have a tendency to be chronic blamers while always viewing themselves as the better parent or the victim. A person with BPD is more likely to project their own misbehavior on you while rallying others to view them as the only victim. Unfortunately, an outside observer is likely to perceive this blame game as two immature people who aren't capable of putting their child first. Your attempts to expose the other parent's outlandish lies may even make you appear unstable, paranoid, and/or malicious.

When separating from a parent with a personality disorder, it is essential to be extremely diligent and cautious as you collect evidence and prepare your case.

Your defense strategy will likely focus on disproving false, unsupported allegations, demonstrating to the courts that you are dealing with a "chronic blamer", and assembling information that proves your true character and consistency. In these scenarios, audio recordings to complement other documented evidence can be especially helpful in revealing their volatile behavior.

Judges will be persuaded more by evidence that demonstrates a series of incidents and patterns of erratic behavior than by your personal diagnosis of the other parent's disorder or mental state.

People in this situation may want to request a Psychological Evaluation for the other parent, but this can be a double-edge sword. First, you will likely have to submit to an evaluation yourself, and second, if the appointed evaluator does not find a personality disorder or is reluctant to categorize a parent's behavior as such, you are left with an evaluation that the other parent can use to assert their mental stability. If a psychologist does conclude with diagnosing the other parent with a personality disorder or expresses concerns for their mental stability, you will still need to prove that their conduct will have a negative impact on the child.

Regardless of your approach, the key is to reveal their concerning behavior through supporting evidence that denotes the relevant symptoms of a disorder. Do not personally assert a diagnosis of the other parent's psychological disorder on the stand. Allow the Judge to come to a conclusion through the evidence you have provided.

Note:

If you suspect that the other parent is exhibiting signs of Borderline Personality Disorder or mental instability, I highly recommend reading the book **_Splitting_** by Bill Eddy LCSW JD. This book can further educate you on this complex situation and guide you on how to best protect yourself during a custody dispute.

PRIVATE INVESTIGATORS

In cases where you have reasonable concerns, but it has been difficult to procure or uncover concrete evidence, it may be necessary to hire a private investigator. This type of detective work may be especially necessary if you suspect abuse, neglect, inappropriate living conditions, or any other situations that may endanger your child and there are no available witnesses.

A licensed private investigator or detective can offer witness testimony in regards to matters that are otherwise very difficult to prove. Although they cannot make recommendations to the court, testimony backed by credible evidence obtained by a qualified PI can be persuasive to Family Court Judges making a ruling in a child custody case.

What can a private investigator uncover?

What needs to be uncovered for each case varies, but the basis of a child custody investigation includes accurate documentation about your child's caregivers and the environment they are exposed to on a daily basis. Common conduct or situations that private investigators look to reveal include:

- Child abuse or mistreatment
- Neglect or other irresponsible conduct with child
- Drug or alcohol abuse while caring for the child
- Revolving caregivers or a parent's lack of time spent with the child
- Criminal behavior or associating with individuals with a criminal background
- Individuals coming and going from the home
- The activity of visitors to and from the caregiver's home
- Infidelity, adultery, or intimate partners in the child's home
- Home environment, items disposed from the caregivers home
- Travel outside the state or to unsuitable or suspicious locations
- Unlicensed, reckless driving, DUI charges
- Lifestyle, daily activities, or schedule
- Parental Alienation or slander
- Hidden assets, income, or employment
- False allegations or claims, fake injuries or disabilities
- Contempt of existing Court Orders

Note:

Court Order violations are a serious offense. Family Courts have modified custody base upon a parent's unwillingness to follow court orders. If you already have a permanent or temporary court order, a Private Investigator may be able to collect evidence that reveals the other parent in contempt of the existing order.

A PI's approach to surveillance and collecting evidence should be centered around the best interests of the child and presenting a strong case for custody.

Note:

Although it is more difficult to detect, proof of Parental Alienation can be a critical factor for judges when determining a custody arrangement. An article about successfully investigating Parental Alienation was written by a PI and can be found in Divorce Magazine - Investigating Parental Alienation Syndrome (PAS).

INVESTIGATIVE METHODS

Family Courts have expressed concerns about testimony from a hired PI whose pay is dependent upon the extent and success of his business. Just as you have the burden of proof, a PI's testimony is also more effective and acceptable as evidence if corroborated by substantial evidence collected during the course of the surveillance. Pictures, artifacts, or videos of the other party engaging in suspicious activity on a consistent basis can be compelling insight that demonstrates the credibility of your PI's testimony.

A suitable PI will have many investigative tools and a network of individuals at their disposal. Depending upon the kind of evidence the PI aims to uncover, their experience and training should allow them to accurately identify which tool is appropriate or necessary to utilize for varying situations. Methods that a PI might implement include:

- Interviews with potential witnesses such as neighbors, co-workers, teachers, other parents
- Criminal background checks on any parties involved in the child's care or home environment
- Video surveillance of a parent's lifestyle or time with the child
- Binocular or Telescopic photos
- Hidden cameras or recorders
- GPS tracking devices
- Tailing or shadowing
- License plate searches
- Internet directory & database searches
- Two-person teams

Note:

Keep in mind that a parent should not engage in any type of surveillance that could be interpreted as an invasion of privacy, harassment, or stalking. Many of the techniques used by Private Investigators require an explicit license to conduct these investigations. Many of the methods listed above are unlawful unless performed by a licensed professional. If you or a PI obtains evidence obtained by illegal means, it will be inadmissible in court and you may be held liable.

HIRING A PRIVATE INVESTIGATOR

Before hiring a Private Investigator, speak with your attorney about your concerns about the other parent. You will want to collectively determine if it's necessary to uncover additional evidence that could be critical to your case. Your attorney may have a recommendation for a well-suited Private Investigator that will be capable of working closely with you and your attorney to build a formative case.

It's also important to know how Private Investigators are viewed by your presiding Family Court. Be cautious of unscrupulous detectives that may have a bad reputation in your district.

Determining who officially hires the PI can be an important decision. If your attorney retains the investigator, any communication, impressions, conclusions, opinions, or drafted documents developed while building your case will be shielded from disclosure by the Attorney Work Product Doctrine. This approach may also protect you from being accused of utilizing a PI to personally harass the other parent.

If you decide to personally hire the PI, be careful not to ask for a referral from mutual friends, neighbors, or coworkers that may accidentally tip off the other parent about the prospective investigation. Schedule interviews with a few PI agencies and bring notes explaining your concerns and details that are important to your case. Be honest when communicating your concerns to your PI - exaggerations and falsities may misdirect your PI and leave you with unnecessary fees and irrelevant information. Inform your PI of the other parent's concerning behavior and your desire to conduct the investigation legally and without your child being impacted.

Characteristics of a qualified child custody Private Investigator

If an investigator is going to play a vital role in the discovery and presentation of evidence for your child custody case, choose one that conducts investigations with high standards of professionalism that are recognized by the Judge. Hiring a PI that presents themselves as professional and objective to the Family Courts may be as persuasive as an expert witness hired to testify in court.

Licensed & Trained

Many states require that anyone employed in the practice of investigation be licensed and bonded to get a PI license. Check if your presiding state has a licensing agency for Private Investigators. These departments offer the education, training, and licensing for PIs and may be able to provide you with a list of local professionals that are certified with current licenses in good standing with that agency.

Specializes in child custody cases

A private investigator that specializes in child custody cases will know the rules of evidence, understand the Custody Factors, and how to substantiate them with relevant evidence. Above all, they will ensure that the child's well-being is the priority of the investigation.

Credibility with the Family Court System

A professional and untarnished reputation with the Judges in your district is important. Integrity and ethics are substantial in the eyes of the court, while previous misconduct can nullify all the effort and work performed during the investigation.

Experienced on the stand

A PI that is familiar and comfortable with presenting testimony and answering questions while under pressure on the stand can be as important as the evidence itself.

Skilled, focused, and organized

Skilled at tracking, researching, and documenting while maintaining focus on relevant matters. Their work should be organized and presented clearly with accurate chronicling of events.

Charismatic and a strong network

A charismatic PI will have the ability to put people at ease and extract valuable details with good interviewing skills. A strong network in the local community can allow for greater access to relevant resources or leads that might otherwise be difficult or impossible to obtain.

Familiar with behavioral patterns

Having an intuitive nature and quick reasoning skills will assist them when identifying or tracking specific behavioral patterns. They are more likely to predict the moves or decisions of others, making for a more efficient investigation.

Persistent, but patient

A good investigator has a balance of persistence and caution, keeping their operation concealed while maintaining opportunities for capturing quality evidence. Extra care must be taken by you and the investigator to not leave tracks or tip off the other party.

Reliable

A PI that is punctual with his assigned surveillance and has communicated to you the best means of reaching him. It is important that is not difficult to contact your PI and responsive to your calls or emails that could assist their investigation.

Familiar with the location of investigation

An investigator who can easily navigate the area and identify likely points of interest will make for a more efficient operation. They will be able to anticipate certain routes, avoid traffic, and be strategic when selecting a location for observation.

If you are trying narrow down your selection of a well-suited PI for your case and your attorney cannot assist, check with the American Society of Industrial Security or the National Association of Legal Investigators. They may be able to inform you if any of your selected PIs are affiliated with their nationally accredited organization.

TIMING

Ideally, an investigation will be initiated before a custody complaint has been filed. Evidence will be more difficult to gather if the other party is on guard or behaving cautiously. If you can present a case that is supported by credible and relevant evidence collected during the initial phases of the custody dispute, it may help expedite an early settlement.

The time directly after the other party has been served with a custody complaint may prove to be opportune for conducting surveillance while emotions are charged, adjustments are occurring, and decisions are more likely to be made impulsively.

WHAT DOES IT COST?

The factors that influence the cost of a Private Investigator are:

- Hourly rate
- Time spent
- Effectiveness vs chance
- Your management of the budget

Competent investigators can be expensive and rates vary depending on the investigator and their level of service, but typical PI rates range from $50-$250/hour, depending on your area. Plan on spending at least $500-$2500. There are some agencies that offer set project rates for certain cases. For example, an agency may offer two 8-hour investigative days for a set fee of $1600. If a lot of travel is necessary to gather useful evidence, expect to pay an even higher rate.

Occasionally, brief investigations can reveal mistreatment, but extensive surveillance is often required to establish a pattern of abuse, neglect or unwarranted behavior on a consistent basis. Determine the level of investigative service you can budget into your overall cost of litigation. If your budget is small, determine preset limits and offer them insight on favorable hours or timeframes for the most effective surveillance.
Ask for a cost estimate, the hours they estimate for your situation, and check-in points. If you proceed with initiating the investigation, always get a written and signed contract that specifies the purpose of hiring the PI, the rate, and the services you will receive.

PRIVATE INVESTIGATOR: FINAL NOTES

Professional investigative services can often assist with gathering evidence, but there is no guarantee that they will be able to obtain the information you are seeking. Regardless of the amount of work an attorney or PI puts towards your case, your personal preparation is paramount. The majority of supporting evidence should be collected and organized by you.

DISCOVERY & DISCLOSURE

Before a case goes to trial, parties have the right to request copies of evidence that the other party has in their possession that could be relevant to the case. This right to disclosure, is analogous to forcing the other party to show their "cards", but not their strategy. Some information is mandatory as part of the court filing process (basic facts such as names, birth dates, residence, and income), which means this information must be provided to the opposing party without them specifically requesting it. Other information must be specifically requested or "discovered", which means the information must be provided, whether or not the evidence will be used in court by the disclosing party, but only if requested through the discovery process. Evidence should be differentiated from theories or case strategies that are developed.

Discovery refers to the procedures by which each party learns about evidence that the other party does not automatically have to disclose as part of the proceedings, but they cannot be used to elicit privileged communications. The discovery process usually happens in the pretrial phase of a lawsuit where each parent can make a "request for evidence" (RFE) from the opposing parent by means of discovery devices including:

Request for answers to interrogatories

A request for further information through a formal set of written questions. This device is used in an effort to determine matters of fact in advance of trial and disputed matters that will require a counter-response. The respondent only needs to answer to matters within their personal knowledge. Objections to the validity of a question can be raised unless the court determines the question relevant to the case.

Request for admissions

Also known as a request to admit, includes statements or claims submitted by the opposing party for the purpose of having the parent admit or deny the statements. This request can be made within initial pleadings or after a parent has been served. If the opposing party fails to respond or object in a timely manner, the allegations are automatically deemed admitted. As a result, the court process can be more efficient by establishing what matters are agreed upon and what matters are disputed before the trial date.

Request for production of documents

A request for tangible evidence such as documents, electronic communications, recordings, or images that may be relevant to the case.

Depositions

This discovery device is an oral examination of a party or witness. The session is taken under oath and is considered committed testimony, which may be used at trial.

Although a Judge will not be present, the questioning session is recorded by a court reporter and may also be videotaped.

During a deposition, your attorney will seek to determine the other parent's story before the trial, in an effort to develop a defense. Your attorney can also use the testimony obtained during a deposition to catch a parent or other witness in a lie on the stand or in their pleadings, which can jeopardize their credibility with the Judge.

Note:

If you are required to take deposition, proper preparation is essential. Your answers given under oath should be consistent with your pleadings and testimony in court. If you have been instructed to produce supporting documents for the deposition, bring three copies. One for the opposing counsel, one for yourself, and one that will be kept by your attorney. To save time and attorney fees, you can apply this approach to all documents you plan to present as evidence.

After the discovery process has been initiated, each party must voluntarily provide additional evidence or witnesses as they become known, unless the information is legally privileged or proven overly burdensome to produce. If a party fails to provide evidence that should have been disclosed in a timely manner, the Judge may not allow the party to use that information at trial.

When responding to interrogatories, admissions, or deposition questions, be concise. Do not provide more information than necessary to assert or correct the facts. Some questions require a simple 'Yes' or 'No' and others may need additional explanation.

Pay attention to what kind of information each question is requesting of you. Elaborate explanations will be further questioned, create doubt, or ensue an "appearance of defensiveness".

Privileged Communication & Rule of Confidentiality

The Privilege Rule allows certain private communications to be kept in confidence and protected from discovery. These protected relationships assist a professional (such as an attorney) in providing a safe environment that promotes full disclosure of information to the benefit of the client. The most common privileged communications are those between clergy and communicant, psychotherapist and patient, physician and patient, and attorney and client.

> *When communicating with your attorney through email, never cc: the opposing party. If you do so, you waive the attorney-client privilege.*

The attorney–client privilege protects confidential communications between a client and their attorney for the purpose of legal advice. In order to secure effective representation, a client must feel free to discuss all aspects of a case without fearing that their attorney will be called at trial to repeat their statements.

Note:

Privileged communications are not always absolute and can be arguable in Family Court on the grounds that they exclude relevant facts that may assist the Judge in a child custody determination. Since the traditional rules of evidence are more relaxed in Family Court, Judges may rule on evidentiary objections with broader discretion.

For instance, a party may be able to subpoena private communications between a patient and their therapist, if the opinion of the court or the best interests of the child outweighs the interest of confidentiality. If you believe there could be material evidence that may fall under the protections of privilege, talk to your attorney about what can be subpoenaed in your presiding state.

The Attorney Work Product Doctrine

The Attorney Work Product Doctrine protects statements, notes, reports, documents, and other materials or theories developed during an investigation or in the course of preparing for litigation. In other words, it protects a lawyer's capacity to prepare for a case by removing the threat of the opposing counsel discovering their case's strategy. Most importantly, this confidentiality allows the attorney, clients, and private investigators to communicate freely in preparation for trial.

TIMING & STRATEGY

A party's timing and amount of evidence or strategy revealed during each phase of a custody case can have a significant impact on negotiations, litigation, and the outcome of the case. Your timing of evidence disclosure and filing of papers can also affect the other party's preparedness to counter, explain, or defend their case. Unless a discovery has been initiated, you should avoid disclosing your evidence or case's strategy to the other parent.

Despite the assistance of discovery devices, an opposing party's inability to conceive of every possible question may result in a significant gap in the information understood and possessed by each party. Although a party has the duty of disclosure if requested, the rules of confidentiality and attorney-client privilege enable them to conceal their case's strategy. An experienced attorney will guide your case with carefully crafted responses, limited testimony, and prudent timing of disclosure.

During the initial and heated stages of a child custody dispute, you may be tempted to disclose evidence to tout your position, intimidate the opposing party, or get an upper hand in negotiation; however, if not timed appropriately, the impulsive unveiling of information may escalate the tension, help your opponent prepare, or even encourage false accusations that further complicate matters.

Before leading on about your strategy or what evidence you have available, discuss tactical dissemination with your attorney. The drawbacks of educating the other parent too early about your strategy should be weighed against the potential benefit of surprise.

FINAL WORDS

Your child's future depends on your capacity to prepare a case that accurately demonstrates your capabilities and commitment as a parent. Many child custody cases are settled without the additional time and expense of evaluators, depositions, private investigators, or lengthy trials, but with such high stakes, it is essential that you are ready for any possibility. If your case does make it to trial, the actual time in front of a Judge will be brief and the outcome will be greatly influenced by the evidence provided. Thus, the key to prevailing is understanding the Custody Factors used by Family Courts, gathering relative evidence, and organizing it strategically for your case.

Fathers who prepare properly and actually fight for child custody, not only show the courts their commitment to being in their child's life but are often awarded an equal custody arrangement, if not more. By implementing the strategies in this book, you will be more prepared than 90% of other parents, avoid costly mistakes, and move closer to securing a fair settlement that honors your role as their parent.

Made in the USA
Las Vegas, NV
23 December 2023

83486960R00049